Revealing the Unknown God

Steve Wolf

Revealing the Unknown God
ISBN: 0-9800-9072-5
ISBN- 13: 9780980090727
Copyright © 2011 by Steve Wolf Ministries

Unless otherwise indicated, all Scripture quotations are taken from the *New King James Version*. Copyright © 1982 by Thomas Nelson Inc. Used by permission. All rights reserved.
Printed in the United States of America.
All rights reserved under International Copyright Law.

CONTENTS

Introduction..v
1. The Great Need...1
2. You've Heard It Said, But I Say to You....................7
3. The Father Concealed..11
4. The Father Revealed..17
5. The Meaning of Life..31
6. The Gifts We've Been Given.................................41
7. Purpose..73
8. Family..83

Prayer to Receive Salvation..93
Prayer to Receive the Baptism
of the Holy Spirit..95

Introduction

The purpose of this book is to give the reader a true and accurate revelation of God. As the author, my goal is to be in perfect union with the Holy Spirit and write as He leads me. The Word of God is living and powerful. This book is full of scripture, therefore, full of life and power. I trust that the Holy Spirit will bear witness to the truths contained in this book.

I can confidently declare that no one will be the same after reading this book. How can I be so sure? Because I know that when the true character and nature of God is revealed, His love will melt even the hardest heart. If you don't want to read a book that actually has the potential to change your entire life, then you should put this one down. However, if you are ready to receive all that God has for you, keep reading. I pray that grace and peace be multiplied to you through the knowledge of Him who called you.

Chapter 1
The Great Need

Every single day there are people who make a decision to reject God. I believe the majority of these people are actually rejecting a distorted, false, and inaccurate representation of who God is. Sadly, today's churches bear most of the blame for misrepresenting the true character and nature of God. They are zealously preaching and proclaiming a God that they barely even know. It is not enough to believe that there is a God. "*You believe that there is a God. You do well. Even the demons believe—and tremble*" (James 2:19). A basic knowledge that God exists isn't enough for salvation. You have to know God. "*Then Paul stood in the midst of the Areopagus and said, "Men of Athens, I perceive that in all things you are very religious; for as I was passing through and considering the objects of your worship, I even found an altar with this inscription: TO THE UNKNOWN GOD. Therefore, the One whom you worship without knowing, Him I proclaim to you*" (Acts 17:22–23).

I'm not saying that the modern church is as bad as the Athenians, but for the most part, they are trying to worship a God they do not know. You might think it is wrong for me to say that someone doesn't know God, so I offer these examples. Anyone who would get up in front of a congregation and tell them that God might put sickness on them or bring tragedy into their life to teach them a lesson, does not know God. If they say that God wants you poor, they don't know God. If they say God is keeping track of, and judging you for each individual sin you commit, they don't know God. Anyone with a close intimate relationship with God would be quick to denounce such heresies because they know the true character and nature of God. If these statements shock you, I would recommend reading my first book *Church Can Ruin You and Religion Can Kill You*. It counters these and other popular religious traditions of man with the truth and sets people free.

I believe one of the greatest needs of the world today is for Christ's body, which is the church, to be ambassadors for Christ. When you are an ambassador, you deliver the message you were sent to deliver, not your own message. The gospel of Jesus Christ, the true gospel, is the power of God unto salvation (Rom. 1:16). It is a simple message and it hasn't changed. Every born-again believer has been commissioned to take the message of God's unconditional love and grace to the world. If it is so simple, then why is it that there are so many churches spreading false doctrine, wrong teaching, and basically giving God a bad name? The answer: people.

People are goofy! Here's something to think about: Jesus wasn't a Baptist, Paul wasn't a Catholic, the Apostles weren't Lutheran, and Timothy wasn't a Methodist. So what happened? Why is there so much disunity in the body of Christ? The Bible hasn't changed. The gospel hasn't evolved. Contrary to popular opinion, God hasn't slowly revealed His Word to us like when you peel back layers of an onion. The mystery of the gospel was revealed over two thousand years ago (Col. 1:26).

Anyone who has had access to a Bible, has had the fullness of the gospel available to them. But sadly, most people would rather take the word of a preacher as truth than make the effort of searching the scriptures themselves to verify the message being preached. If every Christian of the past would have placed the proper value on reading, studying, and meditating on the Word of God, the body would not be in the divided state that it is in today. Imagine how bad it looks for unbelievers to see such disunity created by so many denominations. Have you ever looked up "churches" in your phone book? How many categories does your city have? How can this be since most of us clutch the same book on the way into church? Once again, the answer is people.

People created denominations. They are not of God. The Apostle Paul spoke against this: "*Now I say this, that each of you says, 'I am of Paul,' or 'I am of Apollos,' or 'I am of Cephas,' or 'I am of Christ.' Is Christ divided? Was Paul crucified for you? Or were you baptized in the name of Paul?"* (1 Cor. 1:12–13). God has always desired for us to "*endeavor to keep the unity of the Spirit in the bond of peace*" (Eph. 4:3). Psalm 133:1 says, "*Behold, how good and how pleasant it is for brethren to dwell together in unity!*"

Simply put, denominations were created by people to make the Word of God line up with their belief system, instead of making their belief system line up with the Word of God. You could say that the word "denomination" is just a fancy word for "excuses." Many were created for the sole purpose of explaining to people why the Word doesn't say what it says. Others were formed to dismiss the power spoken of in the New Testament for every Christian as "not for us today." A great number make excuses as to why we're not getting the results the Word says we should. Finally, and perhaps worst of all, there are denominations that slap Jesus in the face by saying that the great price He paid for our complete and total salvation was not enough, and we have to add to it with our good works or various religious duties.

The large signs displayed in front of churches proudly declaring that church's denomination should be re-written. They should actually say, "We only believe certain parts of the Bible, come inside and find out which parts we reject." There are certain scriptures you'd be hard pressed to ever hear in some of these churches. Mark 16:17–18 is just one example. "*And these signs shall follow those who believe: In My name they will cast out demons; they will speak with new tongues; they will take up serpents; and if they drink anything deadly, it will by no means harm them; they will lay hands on the sick, and they will recover.*" Among other things, this passage of scripture tells us that those who believe or "believers" will have signs following them. Verse 20 says, "*And they went out and preached everywhere, the Lord working with them and confirming the word through the accompanying signs.*" Another tough scripture to get around is John 14:12. "*Most assuredly I say to you, he who believes in Me, the works that I do he will do also; and greater works than these he will do, because I go to My Father.*" This gospel that we should be preaching demands results. You'd have to read your Bible in bits and pieces to come up with a different conclusion.

So, rather than bear the burden of results, denominations were created to explain away the truth; to water down the message; to choke out the power. Christians have let religious traditions of man creep into the body of Christ, bringing condemnation and a spirit of timidity that renders many parts passive and altogether useless. Jesus said that a kingdom divided will not stand. The body of Christ divided will only get limited results. I believe the great need of our day is unity of the church. I believe a revelation of the true character and nature of God is the first step. It is only then that a close intimate relationship with God through Jesus Christ can be pursued.

Chapter 2
You've Heard It Said, But I Say To You

Before Jesus went to the cross, He appeared before Pontius Pilate and was asked many questions because he knew that Jesus wasn't deserving of death. *"Pilate therefore said to Him, 'Are You a king then?' Jesus answered, 'You say rightly that I am a king. For this cause I have come into the world, that I should bear witness to the truth. Everyone who is of the truth hears My voice.' Pilate said to Him, 'What is truth?'"* (John 18:37–38). For the most part, our society has thought of truth as something that is relative or open to interpretation. Often facts are mistaken for the truth. 2 Cor.5:10 *"...while we do not look at things which are seen, but at the things which are not seen. For the things that are seen are temporary, but the things which are not seen are eternal."* Facts are temporary and subject to change. Truth, however, is eternal; it will not change. *"Jesus Christ is the same yesterday, today, and forever"* (Heb13:8

He does not change. "*The grass withers, the flower fades, but the word of our God stands forever*" (Isa.40:8).

Here is an example of facts vs. truth. Let's say you've been diagnosed with cancer by a very reputable doctor—a specialist. He will be able to prove to you with X-rays, tissue samples, etc., that your body has cancer. That would be an undeniable fact. However, facts are subject to change. Now, here's the good news; here's the truth. Over two thousand years ago Jesus took that sickness on His body. "*He Himself took our infirmities and bore our sicknesses*" (Matt. 8:17). "*He was bruised for our iniquities; the chastisement of our peace was upon Him, and by His stripes we are healed*" (Isa. 53:5). In this example, you would now have to make what could be a life or death decision. Are you going to believe the report of the doctor, or are you going to believe the report of the Lord? Whose report carries more weight with you? Are you going to accept what your eyes see, what your body feels, or what your ears hear as truth? Or are you going to believe Jesus—the Way, the Truth, and the Life?

Everyone must reach a point in their life where they ask themselves: what do I believe? Your personal belief system can either: oppose the Word of God, agree with the Word of God on certain points, or completely line up with the Word of God. I call them personal beliefs, because when it comes down to it, what you believe is your choice. People will try to influence your beliefs or try to sway you to accept their beliefs. It starts with your parents, then your teachers, your friends and family, your pastor, and even your TV. When you take all this into account, you can see how a person's belief system could be quite complex and unique. There would be no absolute truth. It doesn't have to be that way. You can do what I did and choose to believe the gospel. I believe the Bible is the inspired Word of God Almighty. If you believe that too, then you must believe that either it is all true, or none of it is true.

God's ways are perfect and His Word is proven (Ps.18:30). God is not a man that He should lie (Num. 23:19). If one single scripture in the Bible could be found untrue, then we would have to throw it all out. Even God Himself declares that He framed the world by His spoken words. He is so convinced of their eternal power that "*He upholds all things by the word of His power*" (Heb. 1:3). I challenge anyone to place their finger on any part of the Bible that is untrue. We need to do what is prescribed in Romans 3:4 and "*let the word of God be true and every man a liar.*" One reason the Word of God is so living and powerful is because it is absolute truth. Ps. 138:2 "*For You have magnified Your word above all Your name.*" There is nothing that God exalts higher than His Word. "*In the beginning was the Word, and the Word was with God, and the Word was God*" (John 1:1). Jesus is the Word. "*And the Word became flesh and dwelt among us*" (John 1:14). "*It pleased the Father that in Him all the fullness should dwell, and that in all things He should have the preeminence*" (Col. 1:19). Since God gave His Word preeminence (to be supreme, first, have first place), we should also place His truths above people's beliefs. We must also place it above religious traditions of man and let nothing or no one be exalted above the Word of God.

A phrase often repeated by Jesus was, "You've heard it said, but I say to you." It is with this same attitude that I write this book. Just because a doctrine is popular and accepted, that doesn't make it true. Even though I'm over two thousand years late, I'm going to answer Pilate's question: What is truth? Truth is every word that came out of the mouth of Jesus. He did not speak of His own accord. He only spoke what the Father told Him to speak. His actions were a perfect representation of God's will. His words were the voice of God. Not a single one of them will return to Him void, but will accomplish what it was sent forth to accomplish. The Word of God doesn't grow old; it doesn't fade or lose its power. It cannot be defeated. It cannot be stopped. No one can stand against it. Not everyone will believe it, but in the end, every knee will bow and every tongue will confess that Jesus Christ is Lord!

Chapter 3

The Father Concealed

There is a great war being waged in America today. "In God we trust" is being pushed out by "Keep God out of the public square." Even our country's undeniable Christian roots are being challenged and ignored. Don't worry, this book isn't going to dive into politics, but I would like to make a few important points. No one could argue with the fact that America has become increasingly secular. The God haters and God deniers have been hard at work since removing public prayer from schools in 1962. I do not, however, believe that the moral decline of our society can or should be blamed on this one event. The church should have used this as a big wake-up call. I believe the elected officials simply mirror our society. A mostly Christian society will elect a mostly Christian government. When the majority of Americans quit basing their voting decisions on the Word of God, but are led by their emotions or pocketbook ... well, look around.

I do not advocate political action as the only or the best tool to bring about reform in our country. Likewise, the Apostle Paul (who lived in one of the most immoral and politically corrupt societies ever) did not advocate political action as the answer. Instead, he told the Christians to submit to government (Rom. 13), and pray for those in authority (1 Tim. 2:1–4). He never waved a political sign, but somehow Christianity swept through the empire until it became the official religion. As Christians, we've been commissioned to preach the gospel. We have to let our voices be heard and our votes counted, but many are trying to put the carriage in front of the horse. When the true gospel is preached, people who receive will have their hearts changed and can change the government with their votes. Government cannot change the moral character of people, only the gospel can.

Why are people so adamant about removing all that is of God and His influence from our society? Could it be that some of the blame should fall on us? "*Let your speech always be with grace, seasoned with salt, that you may know how you ought to answer each one*" (Col. 4:6). Can you say that the church as a whole has been dealing with unbelievers with grace? Or have they been self-righteously dishing out judgment? There's nothing less effective than a religious hypocrite pointing out a person's flaws and telling them that they are such bad sinners. This is not the method that Jesus used. In John chapter 8, the scribes and Pharisees brought to Jesus a woman who was caught in the act of adultery. Knowing that the Old Testament law demanded that she be stoned, they asked Him what He would do. He stooped down and wrote on the ground what was most likely a list of names with lines drawn to known prostitutes. He then said, "*He who is without sin among you, let him throw a stone at her first*" (John 8:7). Well, they all left, from the oldest to the youngest. Finally Jesus remained with the woman. John 8:10-11 "*'Woman, where are those accusers of yours? Has no one condemned you?' She said, 'No one Lord.' And Jesus said to her, 'Neither do I condemn you; go and sin no more.'*" John 3:17 "*For God did not send His Son into the world to condemn the world, but that the world through Him might be saved.*"

There should be nothing shocking about hearing a dog bark. It's a dog. They bark. That's what they do; it's in their nature. Therefore, you should not be shocked to hear that sinners are sinning. They are sinners. That's what they do; it's in their nature. Eph. 2:2–3 says that before we were Christians, we were "*by nature children of wrath, just as the others.*" The lost man can't help but sin, because he has no power to overcome sin nor will he unless he becomes a new creation and receives a new spirit at salvation. Col. 1:13 "*He has delivered us from the power of darkness and conveyed us into the kingdom of the Son of His love.*" Upon salvation, I can say, "*Sin shall not have dominion over you, for you are not under law but under grace*" (Rom. 6:14). "*And having been set free from sin, you became slaves of righteousness*" (Rom. 6:18). We must not beat down or judge a person who is spiritually a slave of sin, having no hope to overcome it. Instead, we should be moved with love and compassion for those "*whose minds the god of this age has blinded, who do not believe, lest the light of the glory of Christ, who is the image of God should shine on them*" (2 Cor. 4:4). The church needs to reveal God's heart to those who are perishing by following Jesus' example of offering them love and grace. We need to preach the good news instead of the "you're no good" news.

There is a worldwide campaign being run against the name of Jesus and God. People have chosen to yield their lives to the enemy for the purpose of this great smear campaign. It is being led by Satan, our adversary, who is the father of lies. "*Be sober, be vigilant; because your adversary the devil walks about like a roaring lion seeking whom he may devour*" (1 Peter 5:8). The good news is he can only devour those who are ignorant of the Word; especially those who are ignorant of the truth that Jesus disarmed principalities and powers. He made a public spectacle of them, triumphing over them in it. Our enemy has been defeated! God gave man dominion over the earth. The only power the devil ever has is when a person yields their authority on this earth to him. Paul warns in 2 Cor. 2:11 not to let Satan take advantage of us, and not to be ignorant of his devices. The way the devil "walks around **like** a roaring lion" shows us that he is a phony, and exposes his devices as fear and lies.

Satan is going to try to get you to doubt the Word of God. He is also going to lie about the true character and nature of our loving Father. He knows that if he can present God as a harsh vindictive judge, or a cruel baby killer, or a destroyer of lives, then no one would want to draw close to Him. This horrific misrepresentation of God, this doctrine of demons, is sadly being spread from many pulpits every Sunday morning. Just like the Athenians Paul encountered, they are trying to worship a God that they do not know. "*But the hour is coming and now is, when the true worshipers will worship the Father in spirit and truth; for the Father is seeking such to worship Him. God is a Spirit, and those who worship Him must worship in spirit and truth*" (John 4:23).

You cannot truly worship God if you are worshipping out of fear of punishment. True worship is not offered to earn right standing with God, or a blessing from Him. If you think worship is something that appeases the great wrath of God in areas you've fallen short, you're missing the whole point. Worship is more of a reaction then anything. When the tender, loving heart of the Father is personally revealed to you, worship will be the reaction. Luke speaks of a certain sinful woman that came to Jesus when He was at a Pharisee's house. She fell at His feet and washed them with her tears, wiped them with her hair, kissed them, and anointed them with fragrant oil. The Pharisee, however, did not offer Jesus anything to wash his feet. Jesus used this woman's act of faith to illustrate that those who have been forgiven much will love much, and those that have been forgiven little would love little. When you realize the depths and totality of your forgiveness, and the great price that was paid for your right standing with the God the Father, you can't help but worship God.

Chapter 4

The Father Revealed

The simplest revelation of God is that God is love. The Bible doesn't say that God has love or sometimes shows love. He is love. We throw the word "love" around so often and use it so broadly, that it has lost its meaning. Our vocabulary doesn't distinguish between loving your spouse and loving ice cream. Obviously we have different degrees of love. The greatest degree of love in natural human terms is defined in John 15:13: "*Greater love has no one than this, than to lay down one's life for his friends.*" I say human terms, because people mostly operate in love based on performance. We show love to the lovely. Matt. 5:44 "*...Love your enemies, bless those who curse you, do good to those who hate you, and pray for those who spitefully use and persecute you.*" Jesus' commandment sounded quite impossible to keep. He goes on to say in verse 46, "*For if you love those who love you, what reward have you? Do not even the tax* *collectors do the same?"* Jesus was highlighting our inability to fulfill the requirements of the law in our own strength. He was also showing that there is a difference between the way God loves and the way people love. We can contrast the Father's love for us in Rom. 5:7–8. *"For scarcely for a righteous man will one die; yet perhaps for a good man someone would even dare to die. But God demonstrates His own love toward us, in that while we were still sinners, Christ died for us."* That scripture says that God demonstrates **His** love.

God loves us with agape love, which is unconditional. Our performance or goodness has no bearing on His love for us. *"For I am persuaded that neither death nor life, nor angels nor principalities nor powers, nor things present nor things to come, nor height nor depth, nor any other created thing, shall separate us from the love of God which is in Christ Jesus our Lord"* (Rom. 8:38–39). We must come to a place where we are completely convinced that God's love for us does not fluctuate with our performance. This is an extremely important foundational truth.

A person would never doubt God's love for them if they meditated on the price that God placed on them. I've heard it said that you can't place a price or value on a human life. That is simply not true, because God clearly placed a value on your life. Before Jesus went to the cross, He spent some time praying in the garden of Gethsemane. He began to ask and plead with God to see if there might be any other way for God to accomplish His plan of salvation for mankind. He asked if it was possible for this cup to pass from Him. Nevertheless, He said, "Not my will, but Your will be done." This is where God placed a value on you. He chose your life over His Son's life. What are you worth to God? You are worth Jesus: God's only begotten Son with whom He was well pleased. God could not place a higher value on you! He told us what the greatest form of love was, and then He demonstrated that love toward you.

I cannot simply say, "God loves you," and that be the end of it. Paul's prayer for the church was that they, "*being rooted and grounded in love, may be able to comprehend with all the saints what is the width and length and depth and height—to know the love of God which passes knowledge; that they be filled with all the fullness of God*" (Eph. 3:17–19). God's love for us is not one dimensional. You cannot read about it on paper and expect to take it all in. God wants us to (experientially) know the love of Christ which passes (mere intellectual) knowledge. Why is this to be sought after? That we might "*be filled with all the fullness of God.*" If we have done what scripture says and "*tasted and seen that the Lord is good,*" who wouldn't want to be "*filled with all the fullness of God*"? We should spend the rest of our lives on this earth searching the depths of His love for us.

You can't give away what you don't have. You can't show God's kind of agape (unconditional) love towards others if you haven't first received it. "*We love Him because He first loved us*" (1 John 4:19). There is an order that we must respect if we are to be effective Christian witnesses. We must abide in God's love until we reach the point that Paul spoke of when "*the love of Christ compels us.*" All the good works that we do that are not motivated by love will profit us nothing (1 Cor. 13:3). When we reach out to a lost world with God's kind of love, it will never fail. It is the chief thing. Even faith works by love (Gal. 5:6). "*And we have **known** and **believed** the love that God has for us. God is love, and He who abides in love abides in God, and God in him*" (1 John 4:6). Notice that you have to first know the love of God before you can believe the love of God. We cannot reveal the one true God to the world without revealing His limitless and unconditional love for them.

It is the goodness of God that leads people to repentance (Rom. 2:4). Satan knows that if he can get people to doubt the goodness of God, he can turn them away. Any teaching or preaching that you hear that causes fear to rise up in your heart must be rejected immediately. Fear, lies, and manipulation are tools of the devil. Love, mercy, grace, and forgiveness are tools of God. "*There is no fear in love; but perfect love casts out fear, because fear involves torment. But he who fears has not been made perfect in love*" (1 John 4:18). A Christian must also recognize that anything, whether it's a sermon, or a feeling, or emotion, that keeps you from coming boldly to the throne of grace is a tool of the enemy. We must at all times know that we can and should run in to the open arms of our Abba (daddy) Father. "*Love has been perfected among us in this: that we may have boldness in the day of judgment; because as He is, so are we in this world*" (1 John 4:17).

Old Testament scripture is one of the biggest obstacles that stand in the way of people perceiving God as being loving. The way God related to people in the Old Testament is completely different than the way He relates to people after Jesus' resurrection. Being able to explain this difference and the reason for it, is one of the most basic duties of a preacher. Paul wrote to Timothy in his second letter: "*Be diligent to present yourself approved to God, a worker who does not need to be ashamed, rightly dividing the word of truth*" (2 Tim. 2:15). Every word of God is true, and all scripture is given by inspiration of God; however, it must be rightly divided.

Before Jesus came and set everyone free, God was dealing with His people on a performance-based system. If the people did good, they were blessed. If the people did bad, or broke one of His commandments, they were punished or cursed. If you want a detailed list of all the old covenant blessings and curses, you should read Deuteronomy chapter 28. The blessings are awesome, and the curses are horrific. You would probably have a hard time believing the same God that I have been describing, the God of love, would actually afflict His people with these curses. Well, He did, so let me explain.

When God first made man, he did not slap a list of do's and don'ts in front of him. The Ten Commandments were not displayed in the Garden of Eden. He simply said do not eat the fruit of this tree. We all know the rest of the story of how Adam and Eve yielded their God given authority over this earth to Satan, thereby allowing sin to enter the earth and cause it to be cursed. It was never God's intention for His creation; man, who was made in His image and His likeness to have to live a miserable life on earth in a cursed state. God immediately set His plan for man's redemption in motion. The salvation of mankind was also God's motive for driving Adam and Eve out of the Garden of Eden. He didn't want them to eat of the tree of life and live forever in their fallen state (Gen. 3:22). It was not anger that drove them out; it was actually love.

When God killed every man and every living thing on the face of the earth that was not with Noah in the ark, He also was acting out of love. God could not save these people that He destroyed, because unlike us, they did not have the option of a new regenerated spirit. They could not be born-again. God saw that "*every intent of the thoughts of his heart was **only** evil continually*" (Gen. 6:5). God knew that at the rate man was going, there wouldn't be a virgin left to bear His Christ. Nor would there have been enough men who could hear the voice of God to prophesy or speak into existence the coming Savior. Remember that God gave man authority and dominion over the earth. Man could do whatever he wanted with it. Sadly, he gave it to Satan. Since God cannot violate His Word, He had to use men to speak through, and a man (Jesus) to get it back.

"*Therefore, just as through one man sin entered the world, and death through sin, and thus death spread to all men, because all sinned. For until the law sin was in the world, but sin is no imputed where there is no law*" (Rom. 5:12–13). God let man walk the earth for roughly 2,000 years without sin being imputed unto him. It wasn't until man began to compare themselves among themselves (Gen. 4:24) that God saw fit to give the law through Moses. It was the attitude of self-righteousness that brought about the law "*that every mouth should be stopped, and all the world may be guilty before God*" (Rom. 3:19).

The Ten Commandments were not given so that people could perfectly follow them. First of all, they were given so that sin could be identified. Rom. 7:7 "*I would have not known sin except through the law.*" Second, it was meant to magnify sin. Rom. 7:8-9 "*But sin, taking opportunity by the commandment, produced in me all manner of evil desire. For apart from the law sin was dead. I was alive once without the law, but when the commandment came, sin revived and I died.*" Rom. 5:20 "*Moreover, the law entered that the offense might abound.*" The whole point of the law was to bring man to the end of himself: to the end of self-righteousness. After that, man's only hope would be to cry out for mercy—for a Savior.

The law was in effect from Moses up until Jesus. During that time, the wrath of God was being poured out against all sin. At that time, sin was being imputed unto man. The people were required to keep the full letter of the law. When they fell short, they had to find a priest and make sacrifices for their sins to avoid the terrible curses named in the law. "*For as many as are of the works of the law are under the curse; for it is written 'Cursed is everyone who does not continue in all things which are written in the book of the law to do them'*" (Gal 3:10). This was truly a fearful time to be alive. God showed mercy to Cain, the first murderer, but had a man stoned to death for picking up sticks on the Sabbath. In 2 Corinthians chapter 3, Paul refers to the Ten Commandments as the ministry of death and the ministry of condemnation. Wow! Are you sure you want that hanging on your wall? (There will be more on that later.)

The old covenant law was temporary, a type and shadow of things to come. When Jesus came, He ushered in a new covenant built on a better hope and better promises (Heb. 8:6). "*Therefore the law was our tutor to bring us to Christ, that we might be justified by faith. But after faith has come, we are no longer under a tutor*" (Gal. 3:24–25). Jesus did not do away with the law or find a way around it. He actually fulfilled the law. "*For *what the law could not do in that it was weak through the flesh, God did by sending His Son ... That the righteous requirements of the law might be fulfilled in us...*" (Rom. 8:3–4). Since the death and resurrection of Jesus, we have been living in the age of the dispensation of God's grace. Why? Because God was mean in the Old Testament, but now He's nice in the New Testament? No—it is because the just and righteous wrath that God had toward sin was placed on the body of Jesus, and He bore it in our place. Therefore God's great and awesome wrath was completely satisfied! "*Much more then, having been justified by His blood, we shall be saved from wrath through Him*" (Rom. 5:9). "*For on the one hand there is an annulling of the former commandment because of its weakness and unprofitableness, for the law made nothing perfect; on the other hand, there is a bringing in of a better hope, through which we draw near to God*" (Heb. 7:18–19).

Who would want to draw near to God if they thought we were still under the old covenant, and God is still pouring out wrath and condemnation every single time we mess up? Can you see why people who don't have a clear revelation of this new covenant we live under would not want to have much to do with God? If you never make the effort to draw near to God, you will certainly be ignorant of His will.

"The Lord works in mysterious ways," has been the slogan for pastors who try to explain difficult circumstances due to their ignorance of the Word of God. Our heavenly Father has absolutely revealed Himself to us. His ways should no longer be mysterious. Eph. 1:9 *"having made known to us the mystery of His will, according to His good pleasure which He purposed in Himself."* Notice that it is God's good pleasure to reveal His will to you. *"The mystery which has been hidden from ages and from generations, but now has been revealed to His saints* [We are New Testament saints: 1 Cor. 1:2]. *To them God willed to make known what are the riches of the glory of this mystery among the Gentiles: which is Christ in you, the hope of glory"* (Col. 1:26–27). When God sent His Son to earth, He also revealed Himself.

Jesus speaking to His disciples said, *"'If you had known Me, you would have known My Father also; and from now on you have known Him and have seen Him.' Philip said to Him, 'Lord, show us the Father, and it is sufficient for us.' Jesus said to him, 'Have I been with you so long, and yet you have not known Me Philip? He who has seen Me has seen the Father; so how can you say, "Show us the Father"? 'Do you not believe that I am in the Father, and the Father is in Me? The words that I speak to you I do not speak on My own authority; but the Father who dwells in Me does the works'"* (John 14:7–10). Jesus goes on in John 10:30 to say plainly, *"I and My Father are one."*

When Jesus walked this earth, He was God

manifested in a human body. Mary, Jesus' mother, carried Him to term, but He was born of incorruptible seed, which is the Word of God, and not of human means. The fact that Mary was a virgin shows us that only God could be the Father. "*In the beginning was the word and the word was with God, and the word was God*" (John 1:1). "*And the word became flesh and dwelt among us...*" (John 1:14). Jesus was like a mirror that reflected the Father. How could we ever question the loving character and nature of our Father? After all, the earthly ministry of Jesus Christ is recorded four different times by four different men in the Bible. None of the other books of the Bible are repeated. When I was a new believer, I often wondered why God would repeat Himself four times. Now, I see the great importance He placed on revealing Himself to the world. I see how he proudly tells and retells His plan for the salvation of mankind.

No one should be ignorant of God's will concerning anything that pertains to this life. "*Therefore do not be unwise, but understand what the will of the Lord is*" (Eph. 5:17). What is God's will concerning salvation? "*...not willing that any should perish, but that all should come to repentance*" (2 Pet. 3:9). "*For whosoever calls on the name of the Lord shall be saved*" (Rom. 10:13). What is God's will concerning healing? "*God anointed Jesus Christ of Nazareth with the Holy Spirit and with power, who went about doing good and healing all who were oppressed by the devil, for God was* *with Him"* (Acts 10:38). *"And great multitudes followed Him, and He healed them all"* (Matt. 12:15). What is God's will concerning your finances? 2 Cor. 8:9 *"For you know the grace of our Lord Jesus Christ, that though He was rich, yet for your sake He became poor, that you through His poverty might be rich."* Gal 3:4 *"… that the blessings of Abraham might come upon the Gentiles in Christ Jesus."* Prov. 10:22 *"The blessing of the Lord makes one rich, and He adds no sorrow with it."* What is God's will concerning your emotions or mental state? 2 Tim. 1:7 *"For God has not given us a spirit of fear, but of power and of love and of a sound mind."* 3 Jn. 1:2 *"Beloved, I pray that you may prosper in all things and be in health, just as your soul prospers."* John 14:27 *"Peace I leave with you, My peace I give you…"*

Now what do you think of my God? I must admit it took me a while to view the Father in the same light as I viewed Jesus. God, in my mind, was more of a stern father figure who was so mighty and powerful that I dared not try to draw near to Him. Jesus, on the other hand, I viewed as my friend as well as loving Savior. He had walked down here with us and knew what this human condition was all about; therefore, I could relate to Him. It took some study and meditation on the scripture before I realized that Jesus was the exact representation of the Father. Now I can call God "Daddy" (Abba) and receive His love and acceptance knowing that He is well pleased with me because of my faith in His Son.

God is on your side. He is for you, and if God be for you, who can be against you? (Rom. 8:31). God knows you to the point that He knows the exact number of hairs on your head. Does that sound like a God who is distant, uninterested or uncaring? His intimate knowledge of us is truly amazing. We must endeavor to do like Paul, and *lay hold of that which has laid hold of us.* 2 Pet. 1:2–3 *"Grace and peace be multiplied to you in the knowledge of God and of Jesus our Lord, as His divine power has given to us all things that pertain to life and Godliness through the knowledge of Him who called us..."* This passage shows us the benefits of knowing God. He alone is good. He alone is worthy of praise and glory and honor. Let the enemy and the world say what they want about our God, but let's receive this great love; this great salvation that He has poured out of His heart into ours. He truly is a good God: His love never fails, His mercy endures forever, His forgiveness is eternal, His Word never fails, and He will never leave you or forsake you. To many, He is "The Unknown God." I promise you He is worth knowing. Draw near to God, and He will draw near to you.

Chapter 5

The Meaning of Life

What is the meaning of life? This question has brought about much speculation and debate. However, I believe it is one of the easiest questions I could answer. How could this be so? Have I obtained a superior mental capacity that dwarfs that of the most educated people? Absolutely not—in fact, if you look at the cover of this book, you'll notice there are no letters after my name. I have, however, made a decision. I have decided to believe God when He said that in Christ are hidden all the treasures of wisdom and knowledge (Col. 2:3). Would you rather have knowledge imparted to you from the thing that was formed—the creature—or from the one that formed it—the creator? "*Let no one deceive himself. If anyone among you seems to be wise in this age, let him become a fool that he may become wise. For the wisdom of this world is foolishness with God*" (1 Cor. 3:18–19).

The Bible contains many examples of God's

wisdom being challenged by the wisdom of this world or man's wisdom. Jesus had to stand and face groups of scribes, Pharisees, and lawyers while they tested His wisdom. "*... the scribes and the Pharisees began to assail Him vehemently, and to cross-examine Him about many things, lying in wait for Him, and seeking to catch Him in something He might say, that they might accuse Him*" (Luke 11:53–54). Not only was He able to answer all their questions and escape all their traps, but He made them look foolish to the point where "*no one was able to answer Him a word, nor from that day on did anyone dare question Him any more*" (Matt 22:46). Stephen, a man that was described as being full of faith and power, also had to face the most highly educated minds of his time. "*And they were not able to resist the wisdom and the Spirit by which he spoke*" (Acts 6:10). Paul was able to escape death many times by speaking with God's wisdom. "*Where is the wise? Where is the scribe? Where is the disputer of this age? Has not God made foolish the wisdom of this world?*" (1 Cor. 1:20)

    I am not against "higher education," as long as a priority is placed on the highest education, which can only be found in the Word of God. "*Do not be conformed to the world, but be transformed by the renewing of your mind...*" (Rom. 12:2). Renewing your mind to the truths of God's Word will cause more success in your health, finances, and relationships than any formal education. Aren't life, liberty, and the pursuit of happiness prerequisites to the "American dream"? Every Christian needs to come to the realization that pursuing what the world defines as success will not bring peace or fulfillment. We need to stop buying what the world has been selling, and unplug from their system. The pursuit of happiness will always be just that: a pursuit. Happiness comes and goes as it is tied to your outward circumstances. The American dream tells us that if we get a good education, then we get a good job, a good spouse, and a nice house where we park our nice cars and raise our fine kids. Finally you have arrived; happiness is yours! Oh, wait, did you get the latest and greatest flat-screen TV?

Don't get duped into running the rat race. If I were to ask parents of young children, "What one thing would you want your child to have in life?" a common answer would be: "I just want them to be happy." Well, I have found something better than happiness. It is called joy, and can only be found in the Lord. "*You will show me the path of life; In Your presence is fullness of joy; at Your right hand are pleasures forevermore*" (Ps. 16:11). It stands to reason that in the Lord's presence there is fullness of joy because Jesus was described as being anointed with the oil of gladness above all His companions. "*These things I have spoken to you, that My joy may remain in you, and that your joy may be full*" (John 15:11). Being full of joy all the time and in the midst of every circumstance is just one of the many fruits of salvation.

Salvation is also the starting point when discovering the meaning of life. If you haven't done so already, you need to surrender the reins of your life to our loving Father. God made you, and He knows your likes and dislikes. He's also called you and given you gifts to fulfill your calling. Everyone has a call of God on their life, but not everyone answers the call. If you do, you will find yourself in a life of fulfillment. Only God can show you the specific race He created you to run; trying to do your own thing and run your own race will always lead to disappointment and a sense of lack. God will take much better care of you than you could ever for yourself. Let God be the Lord of your life.

Finally, I will reveal the meaning of life as it was revealed to me by the Author of life. Let me first answer the most basic questions: Why did God create mankind? Why are we here? "*God created man in His own image, in the image of God He created him; male and female He created them*" (Gen 1:27).Why did God desire to create man in His image and likeness? Man was the pinnacle of all His creations. God already had millions of angels about His throne (Rev. 5:11). If He desired more servants, He would have created more angels. God, however, wanted more than servants, and more than creatures. Have you ever tried to have a conversation with a cat? Hopefully it was a very one-sided conversation. We were created after His image and likeness so that we could relate to God. He desired family and close, intimate, personal relationship. Gen 3:8 shows us that He used to walk and talk with man in the cool of the evening. We were created for God's pleasure (Rev. 4:11). Also, God gave man a kingdom to rule over (earth) much like the way He ruled over His kingdom (heaven). God set man over the earth to fill it up and subdue it; to have dominion over all the earth and every animal and every living thing in it (Gen. 1:26–28). His original design was to give man God-like authority over the earth. This also points back to relationship, because we all know it is easier to relate to a person who shares the same field or occupation as you.

When Adam and Eve allowed sin to enter, they lost their God-given authority and it immediately affected the one thing that God held most dear: their relationship. The first thing Adam and Eve did was withdraw from God by hiding themselves. God did not withdraw from man, as the Bible records conversations He had with Adam's son Cain. After Cain killed his brother Abel he told God, "*I shall be hidden from Your face*" (Gen.4:14). "*Then **Cain went out** from the presence of the Lord...*" (Gen. 4:16). Sin was affecting man's heart toward God. Gaining the knowledge of good and evil brought in sin consciousness and, therefore, self-condemnation. In order to restore the original purpose of man's existence (close, intimate relationship), God had to remove this barrier of sin. The finished work of the Lord and Savior Jesus Christ magnificently accomplished this great task. "*Now all things are of God, who has reconciled us to Himself through Jesus Christ*" (2 Cor. 5:18).

So, how does our salvation factor into the meaning of life? Let me explain by using the most recognized scripture in the Bible. John 3:16 "*For God so loved the world, that He gave His only begotten Son, that whosoever believes in Him shall not perish, but have eternal life.*" Here is the way most people have interpreted this scripture: If you believe in Jesus, you will not go to hell, but live forever in heaven. That statement is true, but that is not what this scripture says. Everyone is going to live forever whether it's in heaven or hell. Let's see how Jesus defined eternal life. "*And this is eternal life, that may know You, the only true God, and Jesus Christ whom You have sent*" (John 17:3). Jesus described eternal life as knowing God and knowing Him.

It sounds too simple, but this is also the meaning of life, or the purpose of our existence. Let's go a little deeper. The word "know" used there (*ginosko* in the Greek) goes beyond an intellectual level. It refers to an experiential, personal, and intimate understanding. The same word is used in Luke 1:34 when Mary said, "*How can this be since I do not know a man?*" Therefore, Jesus defines eternal life as having a close, personal, and intimate relationship with God through Him. Eternal life is a present tense reality for a believer, and not something that will take place in the sweet by and by. "*He who believes in the Son **has** eternal life*" (John 3:36) "*Most assuredly I say to you, he who hears My word and believes in Him who sent Me **has** eternal life*" (John 5:24). With this in mind, let's reread John 3:16. "*For God so loved the world, that He gave His only begotten Son, that whosoever believes in Him shall not perish [die spiritually] but have [present tense] eternal life [close, personal, intimate relationship with God].*" We can see that the forgiveness of sins is not the point of salvation, but intimacy with God the Father is. Therefore, anyone who preaches salvation as only forgiveness of sins, and stops there, is missing out on eternal life (which is the whole point).

I believe the reason we see so many Christians get saved and then "stuck" is because of the way salvation was presented to them. Most people become a Christian so that they will not go to hell when they die. Although that is a good reason, avoiding hell should not be the goal of salvation. If the church presents the goal of salvation as having your sins forgiven and securing a place for yourself in heaven, then once you have responded to an altar call and received salvation, that's it. You've reached the goal! There's no point in going to church, reading your Bible, or growing with God. Hopefully you can see that the goal of salvation is a close, intimate relationship with God through Jesus Christ.

"*And this is the testimony: that God has given us*

eternal life, and this life is in His Son. He who has the Son has life; he who does not have the Son of God does not have life" (1 John 5:11–12). Are you alive the way the Bible describes it? If not, technically you are dead. That's bad news, but the good news is anyone who has been born again has passed from death into life (1 John 3:14). Simply put, you are either a child of darkness or a child of light. There is no grey area concerning this. You either have the Spirit of Christ inside of you or you don't (Rom. 8:9). "*Therefore, if anyone is in Christ, he is a new creation; old things have passed away; behold, all things have become new*" (2 Cor. 5:17).

    Is there anything more desirable than being "in Christ"? Your career, your family, and your material possessions all pale in comparison to being found "in Christ." The Apostle Paul put it best when he said, "*In Him we live and move and have our being*" (Acts 17:28). Paul was a man who placed all confidence, priority, and identity in his new nature. Although formerly a well-respected and highly educated religious Pharisee, he regarded all the accomplishments of his former life as dung when compared to the excellency of the knowledge of Jesus Christ. We should have the same attitude knowing that "*we are complete in Him*" (Col. 2:10). "*We have been blessed with every spiritual blessing in the heavenly places **in Christ***" (Eph. 1:3). There is not one need, whether physical, spiritual, or emotional, that won't be met being "in Christ." Remember this: there is not one thing we should place a higher priority on then cultivating our personal relationship with God through Jesus Christ our Lord. Doing this not only fulfills the number one purpose for your existence, but also creates the proper order for a divine flow in every area of your life. "*His divine power has given us all things that pertain to life and Godliness through the knowledge of Him who called us by glory and virtue, by which we have been given great exceedingly and precious promises, that through them you may be partakers of the divine nature*" (2 Pet. 1:3–4).

Chapter 6
The Gifts We've Been Given

The Gift of Salvation

"*He who did not spare His own Son, but delivered Him up for us all, how shall He not with Him also freely give us all things?*" (Rom. 8:32). Hopefully, you have received a deeper revelation of the divine nature of our Father. He is the ultimate giver, and "*gives us richly all things to enjoy*" (1 Tim. 6:13). His gifts and calling are irrevocable (Rom. 11:29). Only a true gift could be irrevocable or without strings attached. None of our gifts, whether large or small, can ever be revoked based on our performance, or they would not have been gifts to start with. It is the very heart of our loving Father to bless us with as many gifts as we will receive. "*Every good gift and every perfect gift is from above, and comes down from the Father of lights, with whom there is no variation or shadow of turning*" (James 1:17). God gives us gifts because He can't help Himself. As long as you've received His first gift (salvation), you are his most cherished and beloved child. Make no mistake, when it comes to His children, God is not a taker, but only a giver.

Every single gift or blessing God has ever given us has been by grace. Mercy can be practically defined as: not getting what you do deserve. Grace, however, means getting what you didn't deserve or earn. Our salvation was a free gift from God completely independent of our goodness or holiness, but rather reflective of His goodness, mercy, and grace. *"For by grace you are saved through faith, and that not of yourselves, it is the gift of God, not of works, lest anyone should boast"* (Eph. 2:8–9). Our part is to believe the gospel, and receive salvation by putting faith in our Savior. God's awesome gift of salvation was free to us, but to Jesus, the price was huge. He was beaten, falsely accused, afflicted, tortured, mocked, despised, rejected, forsaken, and crucified. *"So His appearance was marred more than any man, and His form more than the sons of men"* (Isa. 52:14). Just because salvation is a gift, that doesn't mean we should forget what it cost the giver. In fact, we should acknowledge and receive everything that Jesus died for us to have.

Why would anyone want to neglect so great a salvation? I believe the answer lies in the presentation. If there isn't a clear presentation of true salvation, then there won't be any faith to receive it. "*Faith comes by hearing, and hearing by the Word of God*" (Rom. 10:17). How can a Christian ever expect to be an effective witness if they themselves don't have a clear understanding of what salvation means. Are you saved? What's saved? The Greek word used for "saved" in the New Testament is "*sozo*." It is a verb and means: to save, rescue, deliver, heal, and to make whole. This simple revelation shows the totality of our great salvation. Let's reread Eph. 2:8–9 in this context. "*For by grace you have been* [saved, healed, delivered, made whole] *through faith, and that not of yourselves; it is the gift of God, not of works, lest anyone should boast.*" We must be careful not to deny the entirety of Jesus' accomplished work by elevating only one aspect of our salvation. If you believe that Jesus died for the forgiveness of your sins, you must also believe that the stripes that were laid on Him were for the healing of your body. Why stop short? Why only believe a partial gospel?

The scriptural accounts of physical healing being part of Jesus' atonement are overwhelming. Isaiah 53:4–5 prophesies of what Jesus' sacrifice would accomplish for us. The word is confirmed in Matthew 18:16–17: "*And He cast out the spirits with a word, and healed all who were sick, that it might be fulfilled which was spoken by Isaiah the prophet saying: He Himself took our infirmities and bore our sicknesses.*" This is exactly what Jesus told us to remember when we come together for the

Lord's Supper or communion. Jesus took the bread and said, *"Take, eat; this is my body which is broken for you..."* (1 Cor. 11:24). His body was broken so that ours wouldn't have to be broken. Jesus took the cup and said, *"This cup is the new covenant in My blood..."* (1 Cor. 11:25). This new covenant means total forgiveness of our sins; they are as far away from God's remembrance as the East is from the West (Ps. 103:12). Physical healing and forgiveness of sins are a package deal. Paul said that not properly discerning the Lord's body was the reason there were many weak and sick among the Corinthians (1 Cor. 11:29–30). I have just scratched the surface of the benefits of salvation, but know this: it goes way beyond a "get out of hell free card."

Perhaps one of the greatest miracles that takes place on this earth is when a person receives salvation and is born again. So much is accomplished in the unseen spiritual realm, and it is instantaneous. We are simultaneously given all things that pertain to life and godliness, blessed with every spiritual blessing, and made complete in Him. The person can then look forward to a lifetime of mining out the treasures that were deposited inside of them at salvation. Anyone who has been born again truly lacks nothing. 2 Cor. 5:17 *"Therefore if anyone is in Christ he is a new creation..."* Notice this doesn't say that you were cleaned up or dusted off, but a new creation. Let me explain: You are made up of three parts; you are a spirit, you have a soul (your mind, thoughts, and emotions), and you live in a body. Before you were given a body to live in, or "tent" as Paul called it, God knew you. *"Before I formed you in the womb I knew you..."* (Jer. 1:5). God is the author of life. Despite all the advances of man, he cannot nor will he ever be able to create life from that which is not living. After God formed man out of the dust of the ground, He breathed into His nostrils the breath of life, and man became a living being (Gen. 2:7). Every living thing that is born on this earth has the breath of life in it. Gen. 7:22 makes reference to this when speaking of the flood: *"All in whose nostrils was the breath of the spirit of life, all that was on dry land, died."* It is that human "life breath," that spirit, that keeps a human body alive. James 2:26 says that *"the body without the spirit is dead."*

      Before salvation, you are a spirit, living in a body being kept alive by the breath of life or natural human spirit. At salvation, that natural spirit of life, or spirit of the world actually dies. It is done away with—crucified with Christ. We are now kept alive by a new Spirit that was given to us which is the Spirit of God. *"...He who raised Christ from the dead will also give life to your mortal bodies through His Spirit that dwells in you"* (Rom. 8:11). This is what it means to be born again. Can you see now why God would call us new creations? After we are saved, we will always have the Spirit of God Himself bearing witness with our spirit that we are children of God (Rom. 8:16). That is good news!

Christians should never doubt their salvation since it is a gift that wasn't earned, and certainly can't be unearned. There ought to be a confidence in knowing that the Spirit of God dwells in you, and that He will never leave you or forsake you. *"But you are not in the flesh but in the Spirit if indeed the Spirit of God dwells in you. Now if anyone does not have the Spirit of Christ, he is none of His"* (Rom. 8:9). You are either saved, or you are not. You've either been re-created or you haven't. There's no mystery, no jumping back and forth between saved and unsaved. *"God is a Spirit, and those who worship Him **must** worship Him in spirit..."* The word "must" is used, because God is holy, and when we enter his presence, we have to walk past the veil that Jesus tore in two. We cannot approach God based on who we are in the natural. We must approach God by our new spirit that was created in righteousness and true holiness.

One of the biggest challenges after salvation is seeing yourself the way God sees you. At salvation you are a new creation, old things have passed away, and all things have become new. The first time you looked in the mirror wasn't the change obvious? It probably was not. What became new was the new Spirit that was given to you. This Spirit knows all spiritual truths, is always in tune with the will of God, and is in fact perfect. Our soulish realm (mind, thoughts, and emotions) isn't instantly changed, and must be transformed by the renewing of our minds with the Word of God. This is why the Bible tells us to "work out our own salvation." Your mind is like a computer that was programmed both with the wisdom of the world and the garbage of this world. The more time you spend reprogramming it with the truths of God's Word, the more your thinking and emotions will line up with spiritual truths. When you combine a renewed mind with your perfected spirit, you will see all the promises of God come alive in your life. We must believe in our new identity. We must believe that this gift of salvation recreated our very beings and transferred us from the kingdom of darkness into the kingdom of the Son of His love. This complete and total salvation is truly awesome, and definitely worthy of being shouted from every rooftop. Before you do, wait: the giver of all good things is just getting warmed up. There's more—so much more.

The Gift of Righteousness

Perhaps the most misunderstood yet most practical gift of all is the gift of righteousness. It must be received whole heartedly if we are ever to go deeper in this abundant God- kind of life that Jesus died to give us. Rom. 5:17 "...*those who receive abundance of grace and the gift of righteousness will reign in life through the One Jesus Christ.*" A full revelation of our righteousness comes with so many benefits; it is absolutely necessary for every believer. Understanding righteousness is what opens the door to receive the confidence and boldness that makes Christians effective witnesses on this earth. It is for this reason that the enemy has launched many attacks on these lines. Rest assured, the truth is about to go forth and smash to pieces even the craftiest of his lies. *"In righteousness you shall be established"* (Isa. 54:14).

Since the fall of Adam, there has been a universal cry of man to get back into right standing with God. *"...Because what may be known of God is manifest in them, for God has shown it to them. For since the creation of the world, His invisible attributes are clearly seen, being understood by the things that are made, even His eternal power and Godhead, so that they are without excuse"* (Rom. 1:19–20). Man has free will, but it is obvious that man still has the "fingerprints" of God in his DNA. There is knowledge of God's existence buried deep in the soul of man. Notice how every culture, tribe, or nation of people has at one time tried to worship a god, or multiple gods. It seems that the desire to worship and knowledge of a higher power are universal. The soul of a person will always be restless until it rests in Him. This is how the various religions of the world came about. Simply put, religion is man's attempt to reach God. It is man's attempt to obtain or earn right standing with God. Ultimately, it is man's attempt to satisfy the inborn desire to know God.

Man has invented an innumerable amount of religions and false gods, but when you boil them down;

they are all pretty much the same. They teach that if you follow a certain standard of do's and don'ts, a code of conduct, or tenets, then you can earn through your own self-effort right standing with their god or a ticket to an afterlife or heaven. A popular American philosophy is that as long as you try really hard to be a good person, God will see your heart, grade on a curve, and accept you. The common thread that ties every religion together is that the burden of salvation is placed on the back of the individual. If you are good enough, you will be accepted. *"For they being ignorant of God's righteousness, and seeking to establish their own righteousness, have not submitted to the righteousness of God"* (Rom. 10:3). Earning righteousness based on performance makes sense to the human mind, but all of our self-righteousness is like filthy rags before God. *"For **My** salvation is about to come, and **My** righteousness to be revealed"* (Isa. 56:1).

    True Christianity stands alone. It is different from all other religions. Ours is the only "religion" with a Savior. Christians knew that they would never be good enough to reach God's standard of absolute perfection and received Jesus as their Savior. God knew how futile man's attempt to reach Him through goodness would be, so before the foundation of the world He devised a plan to reach out to man Himself through Jesus. Sadly, there are still plenty of people trying to relate to God based on their performance or adherence to the law. *"For whoever shall keep the whole law, and yet stumble in one point, he is guilty of all*" (James 2:10). Are you up for the challenge? How does perfection only and no room for error sound? Even Jesus said, "*Unless your righteousness exceeds the righteousness of the scribes and Pharisees, you will by no means enter the kingdom of heaven*" (Matt. 5:20). Here, Jesus is magnifying the law to its highest standard. Remember, one reason the law was given was to show man that he was a sinner in need of a Savior.

When we finally stand before the Lord, we must not be like the ignorant majority: begging and pleading to get into heaven, citing all of their good deeds, and thinking that they will be justified because they tried their best or attended church regularly. Instead, we should admit that it is not by works of righteousness which we have done, but by grace we have been saved through faith in Jesus. We should say, "I have a Savior who is a perfect, spotless, sinless sacrifice. Is there an express line I can get in?" Ha ha, thank you, Jesus!

For a Christian, righteousness is not something that must be sought after, pursued, or is finally attained to one day after we mature. The truth is, when you are born again, you are made righteous. "*For He made Him who knew no sin to be sin for us, that we might become the righteousness of God in Him*" (2 Cor. 5:21). Just like salvation, righteousness is a gift that we receive by faith. I was made righteous because I was born-again, and "*put on the new man which was created according to God, in true righteousness and holiness*" (Eph. 4:24).

Righteousness is defined as the state of being in proper relationship with God. I believe I have already established the fact that the only way to have relationship with God is through His Son Jesus Christ. *"For by one man's disobedience* [Adam] *many were **made** sinners, so also by one Man's obedience* [Jesus] *many will be **made** righteous"* (Rom. 5:19). Your wrong actions did not cause you to be a sinner or make you unrighteous. The truth is, everyone since Adam was born into sin, having a sin nature. You were **made** a sinner. Similarly, your right actions, or good works, do not make you righteous. Only by the acceptance of Jesus will you be **made** righteous. This may be contrary to what you've been taught, but that doesn't make it any less true.

I'm sure we've all heard it preached to the unsaved that if they have broken any of the Ten Commandments, then that is what will send them to hell. Although ministers get results from this technique, it isn't true. People do not go to hell for the individual sins they commit. People go to hell for one reason; they reject the payment for their sins which is Jesus Christ. *"Assuredly, I say to you, all sins will be forgiven the sons of men, and whatever blasphemies they may utter: but he who blasphemes against the Holy Spirit never has forgiveness, but is subject to eternal condemnation"* (Mark 3:28–29). The payment that Jesus made for the sins of mankind was so perfect, so complete, that not only has God forgiven Christians of their sins, but He has also forgiven the sins of lost people. "*And He [Jesus] Himself is the propitiation for our sins, and not for ours only, but also for the whole world*" (1 John 2:1). The word "propitiation" is defined as: to appease the wrath of God so that His justice will be satisfied and He can forgive sins. Titus 2:4 "*For the grace of God that brings salvation has appeared to all men.*" Rom. 5:18 "*...even so through one Man's righteous act the free gift came to all men, resulting in justification of life.*" Even though the payment for all sin was made and God has forgiven everyone's sins, people still have to receive the payment for their sins by accepting Jesus as their Savior. However, if they reject Him, they will have to answer for their own sins on that day.

The problem with telling people that their sinful actions made them a sinner is that they will then naturally assume that their righteous actions are what make them in right standing with God. These people will have effectually been put back under the law. "*You have become estranged for Christ, you who attempt to be justified by law; you have fallen from grace*" (Gal. 5:4). The Apostle Paul made a very strong statement when he said, "*I do not set aside the grace of God; for if righteousness comes through the law, then Christ died in vain*" (Gal. 2:21). The enemies of the true gospel, self-righteous religious leaders, will always try to make people focus on their outward actions while neglecting the conditions of their hearts. They fail to see that the "*grace of God ... teaches us that denying ungodliness and worldly lusts, we should live soberly, righteously, and godly in this present age*" (Titus 2:12). It wouldn't be hard to get every pastor of a Christian church to agree that they would like to see their congregation live a life of holy actions, walking in love, and letting Jesus shine through them. However, only those preaching the gospel of God's unconditional love and grace will get the desired results. Only when the pastor has a firm grasp of our new covenant will he be able to minister the power to overcome sin. "*Who also made us sufficient as ministers of the new covenant, not of the letter but of the Spirit; for the letter kills, but the Spirit gives life*" (2 Cor. 3:6). As a church-goer, you have a choice. You can either go to a place that ministers (hands out) death, or a place that ministers (hands out) life.

    Here is an example of a church that ministers death or the law. The pastor perceives that there is a problem with people overcoming sin in their life. He believes the solution is to preach every "Thou Shalt Not" with vigor, fire, and zeal. Fear of punishment and rejection by God are the main motivators used. Guilt and condemnation are the tools of his trade. Sadly, the pastor is not a co-laborer with Christ, who did not come into the world to condemn the world. He is, however, being used by the enemy, because only Satan is the accuser of the brethren (Rev. 12:10). The Bible clearly states that the law is what gives sin its strength. It is foolish to think that preaching more and more of the law would do anything but give people less and less power to overcome sin in their lives. A Christian has been made righteous, and we know that "*the law is not made for a righteous person*" (1 Tim.1:9). "*But now we have been delivered from the law, having died to what we were being held by, so that we should serve in the newness of the Spirit and not in the oldness of the letter* [the law]" (Rom. 7:6). In case you missed it, we have been delivered from the law. "*For sin shall not have dominion over you, for you are not under the law but under grace*" (Rom. 6:14). Pastors who keep their congregation under the law or under the Ten Commandments will always cause them to struggle with sin.

The Ten Commandments are proudly displayed by many churches, and often hang on the walls of a Christian's home. It is out of sheer ignorance that they are displayed. If you are a believer, then you are a New Testament saint. The Ten Commandments were never—I repeat never—meant for the New Testament church. Did Paul encourage the newly formed churches to keep or display them? Absolutely not. In fact, he said, "*And you being dead in trespasses and the uncircumcision of your flesh, He has made alive together with Him, having forgiven you all trespasses, having wiped out the handwriting of requirements that was against us, which was contrary to us. And He has taken it away, having nailed it to the cross*" (Col. 2:13–14). Well, leave it to the church to pry them off the cross and hang them on the wall! The original Ten Commandment tablets are in the Ark of the Covenant along with Aaron's rod and the golden pot of manna. All these items speak of man's rebellion against God. God covered or kept these items hidden from His view with the golden lid, which was the mercy seat, and it was covered with blood. At the cross, Jesus became the mercy seat that was covered by the blood of His sacrifice. Hold on, here's my point, but first, remember that the Ark of the Covenant is a shadow of Jesus Christ, His person, and His work.

In the Old Testament, God slaughtered people for lifting the mercy seat to view its contents (1 Sam 6:19). Can you see God's heart in all of this? He doesn't want the law to be exposed because it will minister only death and condemnation. Do you now see why it is strange to uncover what God kept hidden under the mercy seat? You would have to count the blood of Jesus a common thing, and His sacrifice unimportant. Also, the Ten Commandments were given to the Jews only, and not to the Gentiles. Are you Jewish? Is your church Jewish? Then why adopt a tool that was meant to bring Jews to the end of self-righteousness and into faith in Jesus? *"Therefore the law was a tutor to bring us to Christ, that we might be justified by faith. But after faith has come, we are no longer under a tutor. For you are all sons of God through faith in Christ Jesus"* (Gal. 3:24–26). We need to follow God's example and place His mercy and grace above the law. The goodness of God is the best tool to lead people to true repentance, not the fear of judgment. The only place the law has today is to show a self-righteous **unsaved** person God's standard of perfection, in hopes that they will cry out for a Savior. Since it the ministry of death and condemnation, it has no place in a Christian's life. If you have it on your wall, take it down. You don't need a mirror that magnifies your faults, but rather an accurate reflection of who you are in the Spirit. We have a new and better covenant—believe it!

Let me share with you a vision I had while listening to a sermon on righteousness. When God looks at us, He sees us through the blood of Jesus, and we are holy, blameless, and above reproach in His sight. Satan, however, is going to try to convince us of the exact opposite. I saw a vision of Satan (who was quite puny) beating a Christian who was hunched down on the floor over the head with what looked like a battle axe. I soon realized it wasn't an axe, but the tablets of the Ten Commandments. Well, after a while, his weapon was yanked out of his hand about mid-swing. He just stood there looking at his empty hands, quite confused. I believe God was using this illustration to show me one aspect of the scripture: "*He disarmed principalities and powers*" (Col. 2:15). If Satan can't use the law to condemn you, he is stripped of his greatest weapon. "*There is therefore now no condemnation to those who are in Christ Jesus*" (Rom. 8:1).

Knowing that you are in right standing with God based on your faith in His Son and not on your works should inspire confidence. Knowing you are righteous will allow you to come boldly to the throne of grace. Our faith-based righteousness is such a prevalent theme in the New Testament; I find it incredible that many people miss it. Even David of the Old Testament had a grip on the faith-based righteousness that was to come. "*Just as David also described the blessedness of the man to whom God imputes righteousness apart from works: Blessed are those whose sins are covered; blessed is the man to whom the Lord shall not impute sin*" (Rom. 4:6–8). Romans chapters 3 and 4 both thoroughly explain our faith-based righteousness. I would recommend reading and studying both chapters, but before we move on, let me summarize. "*Therefore by the deeds of the law no flesh will be justified in His sight... But now the righteousness of God apart from the law is revealed*" (Rom. 3:21–22). "*Therefore we conclude that a man is justified by faith apart from the deeds of the law*" (Rom. 3:28). "*Therefore having been justified by faith, we have peace with God through the Lord Jesus Christ*" (Rom. 5:1).

Earlier I referred to the gift of righteousness as one of the most misunderstood yet most practical gift we could receive. It truly is a platform on which all the other gifts can operate. Knowing that you are right with the God who created the entire universe, and that He is for you and nothing can be against you, will inspire confidence. "*Therefore do not cast away your confidence which has great reward*" (Heb. 10:35). If I had to boil down the gift of righteousness to one purpose, it would be this: "*Beloved if our heart does not condemn us, we have confidence toward God*" (1 John 3:21). You cannot have close relationship with someone if you feel that you are unworthy or inadequate. You surely wouldn't want to draw close to someone you thought was angry with you. God knows this, having experienced a people who gave honor to doctrines and ordinances of man while their hearts were far from Him. "*For this is the covenant that I will make ... I will put My laws in their mind and write them on their hearts; and I will be their God, and they shall be My people. For I will be merciful to their unrighteousness, and their sins and their lawless deeds I will remember no more*" (Heb. 8:10–12).

Thanks to this awesome new covenant, a Christian should never feel condemned. God is not keeping an itemized account of all your failures, and neither should you. All the sins you have ever committed or will ever commit have been erased from God's memory by the blood of Jesus. You must establish your heart with these truths. "*Therefore, brethren, having boldness to enter the Holiest by the blood of Jesus, by a new and living way ... let us draw near with a true heart in full assurance of faith, having our hearts sprinkled from an evil conscience and bodies washed with pure water*" (Heb. 10:19-22). Anything that causes condemnation to rise up in your heart is anti-Christ. God, through His Holy Spirit, will always be convicting you of your righteousness; your right standing with Him. God sees you by your born-again spirit, which is as pure, holy, and perfect as Jesus is. "*Love has been perfected among us in this: that we may have boldness in the day of judgment; because as He is, so are we in this world*" (1 John 4:17). Receive abundance of grace and the gift of righteousness, and reign in this life through the one Jesus Christ!

The Gift of the Holy Spirit

Jesus set humanity back on track. "*He abolished death and brought life and immortality to light through the gospel*" (2 Tim. 1:10). He repaired the path of relationship between man and God. He revealed the heart and will of the Father. He disarmed principalities and powers, and gave us the keys to death, hell, and the grave. He gave us the victory that overcomes the world—our faith. Now He is seated at the right hand of the Father where He continually makes intercession for us. However, He left us with another gift that He said would be much better than His bodily presence on earth. "*Nevertheless I tell you the truth. It is to your advantage that I go away; for if I do not go away, the Helper will not come to you; but if I depart, I will send Him to you*"

(Matt. 16:7). Jesus commissioned every believer to go into all the world and preach the gospel to every living thing, but He didn't want us to go out on our own power. Jesus' earthly ministry didn't begin until He received the power of the Holy Spirit, which descended upon Him like a dove. From that day forward, He went out powerful in word and deed, destroying the works of the devil, walking supernaturally among mere men.

The power that is displayed by the Holy Spirit is the final confirmation of the validity of the gospel we should be preaching. If you are not ministering with power, you are not following the example Jesus set for us. Even Jesus commanded His disciples, "*Not to depart Jerusalem but to wait for the Promise of the Father, which, He said, 'You have heard from me; for John truly baptized with water, but you shall be baptized with the Holy Spirit not many days from now'*" (Acts 1:4–5). If you were baptized with water only, then listen up, because this is for you. The baptism of the Holy Spirit is for every believer who will receive. It is the will of the Father for you to be endued with power. "*But you shall receive power when the Holy Spirit has come upon you; and you shall be witnesses to Me in Jerusalem, and in all Judea and Samaria, and to the end of the earth*" (Acts 1:8). Anyone "can" be a witness for God on their own authority or power. However, it is God's plan that we "must" witness with power. "*And my speech and my preaching were not with persuasive words of human wisdom, but in the demonstration of the Spirit and of power, that your faith should not be in the wisdom of men but in the power of God*" (1 Cor. 2:4–5). If this were not true, then only the most educated, well-spoken people with good memories could be effective in pulpit ministry.

One reason Christianity hasn't completely swept the globe is because churches have displayed a form of godliness, but denied the power. The true gospel cannot be preached without there being a demand for results. Many view Christianity as just one of many religions with its own set of creeds, doctrines, and empty words. This is what sets us apart. The words of God are alive and powerful. When they are spoken in faith, the things in this world must submit to a higher order. When a pastor preaches only words and never demonstrates, or proves the things he is saying, he is doing both God and the congregation a huge disservice. Why do you think there are so many atheists and agnostics? They practically beg for someone to show them one shred of proof. Even Jesus said, "*Believe Me that I am in the Father and the Father in Me, or else believe Me for the sake of the works themselves*" (John 14:11).

If Jesus needed to show the power of God to validate the words He was preaching, then why would we think it was optional for us? Instead, people preach a powerless, watered down gospel that varies greatly from the one recorded in the Bible. "*As we have said before, so now I say again, if anyone preaches any other gospel to you than what you have received, let him be accursed*" (Gal. 1:9). People in this world have real problems. They have real needs; they need physical and emotional healing, deliverance, prosperity, and salvation. These needs can only be effectively met by the working power of the Holy Spirit. That's the way Jesus and His disciples did it, that's the way Paul did it, and that's the way we should do it.

Receiving the baptism of the Holy Spirit is like crossing the point of no return. Your eyes will be opened to spiritual truths like never before. However, these revelations also come with responsibility. The baptism has also become a dividing line between churches. Those who believe and receive the baptism of the Holy Spirit are referred to as Spirit-filled churches. The others have chosen to adopt a more convenient theology that denies the ministry and power of the Holy Spirit described in the Bible, dismissing it as "not for us today." It is more convenient because believing this way will excuse powerless living. It's very easy to stay ignorant of God's will and pray, "Lord, please heal me if it be your will." This takes all the responsibility of operating in faith off of the individual.

Realizing the truth that miracles are for today, and that the church can and should be operating in them, will demand some kind of change. So, you can either change your beliefs to line up with the Word of God, or you can deny or twist the scriptures to line up with your beliefs.

The choice is simple. You can either live a powerless life of hit or miss with your prayers sounding more like begging than anything else, or you can receive power to live a victorious life and manifest the mighty name of Jesus to the world.

Before I explain exactly how to receive the baptism of the Holy Spirit, I want to expound on the benefits. The Holy Spirit is a revealer. He will open your spiritual eyes and ears. Jesus referred to Him as the Helper and the Comforter. *"But the Helper, the Holy Spirit, whom the Father will send in My name, He will teach you all things, and bring to your remembrance all things that I said to you"* (John 14:26). For me personally, this has been one of the most prominent benefits. Before I was baptized with the Holy Spirit, I could recall scripture, but it was limited to the memory capacity of my brain. Now, when I am ministering, the Holy Spirit will bring scriptures to my remembrance like a flood. It truly is supernatural in that it is way beyond what I could do with my own intellect. Now let me explain what is meant by *"He will teach you all things."* *"All scripture is given by inspiration of God..."* (2 Tim. 3:16). His Holy Spirit inspired men to write as He directed them.

Who better to teach you things that are written in the Bible than the One who wrote them? Anyone who thinks the Bible is boring or too hard to understand simply needs to receive the baptism. The Holy Spirit's instruction will cause the scriptures to come alive to the point where you truly believe that "*the word of God is living and powerful*" (Heb. 4:12). Once you have tasted and seen that the Lord is good, you can agree that man cannot live by bread alone, but by every word that proceeds from the mouth of God. Oh, to get to the point where His Word burns in your heart like a fire, melting all fear, insecurity, doubt and condemnation. There is such power in the baptism of the Holy Spirit.

It saddens me to see so many Christians struggling to live out a godly life here on this earth. Some say the Christian life is hard, but I say it's impossible. We need help. We need to receive the Helper. With His empowerment, there is not only enough power for victory in every area of your life, but enough to mightily fulfill the specific calling God has placed on your life. Some people are afraid to embrace a life with that much power flowing through them. They know that if they had the power to cast out demons, heal the sick, and raise the dead; they would have a hard time returning to a "normal" or natural life they have grown accustomed to. We have such a distorted view of what a "normal" Christian life should look like. Regularly seeing the miracle-working power of God flowing through us is normal according to the Bible. Jesus said, "*Most assuredly, I say to you, he who believes in Me, the works that I do he will do also; and greater works than these he will do, because I go to My Father*" (John 14:12). How is it that we are able to do these great and greater works? The answer is here: "*because I go to My Father.*" John 16:7 "*It is to your advantage that I go away; for if I do not go away, the Helper will not come to you; but if I depart, I will send Him to you.*" Who would want to refuse a gift that Jesus said He would send to you? Especially when it's a gift that will empower you to live the life He's called you to live?

Don't be afraid to exchange a life of bland, ordinary, and safe for a life of supernatural power—a life of adventure. Do you want to sit idly by watching the enemy destroy the lives of your family and friends while you offer up weak prayers that rarely get results? Wouldn't you rather walk about as a mighty vessel of the Holy Spirit regularly manifesting the power of God and enforcing the victory that was won for us? I wouldn't really know what boldness was if it weren't for being filled with the Spirit. Peter is a good example of the transformation that takes place after being filled. At the last supper, Peter boldly declared, "I will lay down my life for Your sake" (John 13:17). This was spoken out of his own strength. He actually goes on to deny that he was even a disciple of Jesus three times. After receiving the baptism, he boldly stood up and preached to the very people he was so afraid of. He went from totally denying Jesus to: "*Nor is there salvation in any other, for there is no other name under heaven given among men by which we must be saved*" (Acts 4:12). What a huge difference!

It makes sense that since the baptism of the Holy Spirit turns mere believers into powerful and effective witnesses, there is so much opposition and controversy surrounding it. Of course our enemy doesn't want Christians to receive this tremendous power. He will use anything or anyone to keep people from receiving. One popular ploy is to say that you received the Holy Spirit at salvation, and there is no second experience. The Bible, however, teaches the exact opposite.

In Acts chapter 8, Philip ministered to the people in Samaria with the truth and much power. *"But when they believed Philip as he preached the things concerning the kingdom of God and the name of Jesus Christ, both men and women were baptized"* (Acts 8:12).These people were both saved and water baptized. Then, the apostles sent Peter and John to them (notice the second, separate experience), *"who, when they had come down, prayed for them that they might receive the Holy Spirit. For as yet He had fallen upon none of them. They had only been baptized in the name of the Lord Jesus. Then they laid hands on them, and they received the Holy Spirit"* (Acts 8:15–17). These scriptures seem pretty straightforward to me, but since this is so important, here is another example. In Acts 19, Paul found some disciples in Ephesus. He asked them if they received the Holy Spirit when they believed. They replied that they hadn't ever heard that there was a Holy Spirit, and had only been baptized into John's baptism. *"And when Paul had laid hands on them, the Holy Spirit came upon them, and they spoke with tongues and prophesied*" (Acts 19:6).

Speaking in tongues should always follow receiving the baptism of the Holy Spirit. There are plenty of scriptures that back this up, it is my personal experience, and it is what I have witnessed in others. You receive the baptism the same way you received salvation: by grace through faith. If you are a believer, you are qualified—period. It is helpful to recognize that God is well pleased with you because of your faith in His Son, and that it is His good pleasure to give you this powerful gift.

You may flip to the back of this book to find a prayer to receive the Holy Spirit if you want to be baptized right now! You will, however, need to cooperate with the Holy Spirit when speaking in tongues. The Holy Spirit won't hijack your body and force you to speak in tongues. By faith, you start to speak, and the Spirit gives you utterance. It will sound foreign to your ears, or even like stammering. "*For with stammering lips and another tongue He will speak to this people*" (Isa. 28:11). Paul described it well when he said, "*I will pray **with** the Spirit.*" Although you will feel the words rise up, you will have to cooperate and use your voice to speak them out loud. There is nothing scary about tongues; it is peaceful. When I received, it felt like a warm wave of God's love that started at the top of my head and flowed down to the bottom of my feet. What an awesome gift from the Father!

The prophet Isaiah referred to this experience when he said, "*This is the rest with which You cause the weary to rest, and this is the refreshing*" (Isa. 28:12). If you want to talk about the most practical gift that will help you every single day, this is it. Praying in tongues is a refreshing stress reliever. Praying this way allows us to pray directly from our born-again spirit, which has the mind of Christ and knows all things. You can bypass your brain's limited wisdom and draw on the infinite wisdom of God, which was deposited in you at salvation. "*He who speaks in a tongue edifies himself...*" (1 Cor. 14:4). Praying in tongues promotes spiritual growth by building yourself up on your most holy faith (Jude 20). It also allows you to praise God with perfect praise (1 Cor. 14:14) I don't know why anyone wouldn't want to speak in tongues, and I can see why Paul said, "*I thank my God I speak with tongues more than you all*" (1 Cor. 14:18).

The Gifts of the Spirit

I hope I have conveyed the importance, or better yet, the necessity of receiving the baptism of the Holy Spirit. Now, I will expound even further on the giving nature of our God. You could say that the baptism is a broad distribution of the power of God, which He desires all believers to receive. However, with that baptism comes individual gifts that vary from person to person. I don't want to take the time to describe each gift and how it operates, but will offer an overview with this attitude: "*Now concerning spiritual gifts, brethren, I do not want you to be ignorant*" (1 Cor. 12:1). The simple knowledge that you have been given specific spiritual gifts will place you ahead of the majority of believers. There is a gross ignorance of believers when it comes to being able to name the specific gifts God has given them. "*But the manifestation of the Spirit is given to each one for the profit of all*" (1 Cor. 12:7). "*But one and the same Spirit works all these things, distributing to each one individually as He wills*" (1 Cor. 12:11). There are nine gifts listed in 1 Cor. 12:8–10: word of wisdom, word of knowledge, faith, gifts of healing, working of miracles, prophecy, discerning of spirits, tongues, and interpretation of tongues. There are seven gifts listed in Rom. 12:6–8: prophesy, ministry (or serving), teaching, exhortation, giving, leading, and mercy. Finally, Eph. 4:11 lists the five ministry gifts: apostles, prophets, evangelists, pastors, and teachers.

    I believe there are several factors God takes into account when distributing gifts to us as He wills. A person's unique personality, position or stage of life, sphere of influence, and the need around them are factors that can determine which gifts they are given. Even if two people share the same gift, they can minister it in completely different ways. It is an amazing thing to watch a person flow powerfully yet effortlessly in the gift they have been given. This is what it means to be anointed in a specific area. When you are anointed to do something, it means God has given you a specific task, and empowered you to accomplish it. A combination of drawing near to God and recognizing areas in which you have a divine flow, will help reveal the specific gift God has given you.

Once your gifts are discovered, you should flow confidently in them. *"Having then gifts differing according to the grace that is given to us, let us use them"* (Rom. 12:6). However, we shouldn't stop there. 1 Cor. 12:31 tells us to *"earnestly desire the best gifts."* Even Paul desired that the Corinthians *"come short in no gift."* We ought to be good stewards of the gifts we have already been given, and he that is faithful with the least will be given much. *"Even so you, since you are zealous for spiritual gifts, let it be used for the edification of the church that you seek to excel"* (1 Cor. 14:12). Your gifts are not to be used for self-seeking or impure motives. Everything we do needs to be motivated by love and empowered by the Holy Spirit.

I hope this chapter gives you the desire to draw nearer to God. He has given us so much. What good thing has God withheld from us? He truly has given us all that pertains to life and godliness. Does this not also reveal His heart to us? Ask, and it will be given to you; seek and you will find; knock and it will be opened to you. That is a loving God. That is a God worth knowing, and now that you know this, go and tell the world!

Chapter 7
Purpose

We should be walking this earth with a great sense of purpose, looking to Jesus, the Author and Finisher of our faith. *"Being confident in this very thing, that He who has begun a good work in you will complete it until the day of Jesus Christ"* (Phil. 1:6). We have received not only a great commission, but also great empowerment. Therefore, we ought to strive to be good stewards of our gifting and the calling that has been placed on our lives. *"For we are His workmanship, created in Christ Jesus for good works, which God has prepared beforehand that we should walk in them"* (Eph. 2:10). Like Jesus, we should be "about our Father's business." With all that being said, we must, I repeat must, keep the first thing first in our lives. Your personal relationship with God through Jesus Christ trumps everything. You will always find situations or circumstances where the kingdom of God needs to be advanced. These must be met with the power that supersedes natural strength and ability. When you cultivate a close intimate relationship with an Almighty God, you are staying plugged into the power source. Jesus was basically saying the same thing when He said, "*I am the vine, you are the branches. He who abides in Me, and I in him, bears much fruit; for without Me, you can do nothing*" (John 15:5). Christians who are not bearing much fruit are most likely placing other things above their relationship with Jesus. Likewise, Christians who are constantly consumed with doing good works, but have little or no joy, peace, or fulfillment, are also placing other things above their relationship with Jesus.

Time spent in prayer or fellowship with God is never time wasted. I don't care how busy you are, or how important the work is. When you take time to commune with God whether by prayer or reading and studying His Word, you will operate in a divine flow that exceeds working at a natural pace. Tapping into the mind of Christ that is present in your spirit is a sure way to accomplish more in less time. There is nothing more effective than being led by the Spirit of God. It is important to have an eternal perspective on life: "*We do not look at the things which are seen, but at the things which are not seen. For the things which are seen are temporary, but the things which are not seen are eternal*" (2 Cor. 4:18). A spiritually minded Christian with an eternal outlook and a living relationship with the living God is a powerful force on the earth.

"*Therefore, brethren, be even more diligent to make your call and election sure...*" (2 Peter 1:10). Your calling comes with a specific race only you can run. Let us follow Paul's example and "*run with endurance the race that is set before us*" (Heb 12:1). Perhaps we can even share in his testimony: "*I have fought the good fight, I have finished the race. I have kept the faith*" (2 Tim. 4:7). Running your race should not be a dreadful, burdensome task. In fact, you don't even have to do it. No one is going to force you to run. If you want to be saved and then stuck, you can. If you want to follow your own path in life believing you know better than God what's going to bring you fulfillment, that's your choice. I, however, want to encourage you "*that with purpose of heart you should continue with the Lord*" (Acts 11:23).

The truth is, God only made one of you, and He doesn't make mistakes. He is purposeful: a God of order and not disorder. You have a unique combination of age, life experiences, personality, and interests. The way you talk, your sense of humor, all your strengths and weaknesses make you perfect to run your race. Each of us has a sphere of influence that allows us to interact with other people. You can reach people that I can't, and vice versa. With salvation on your lips and healing in your hands, it is vital that you answer the call of God on your life. "*Take heed to the ministry you have received in the Lord, that you may fulfill it*" (Col. 4:17).

Are you a believer? Good choice. Are you a

disciple? Even better. "*If you continue in My word, you are My disciples indeed. And you shall know the truth, and the truth shall make you free*" (John 8:31–32). True faith in the gospel of Jesus Christ produces salvation. However, being a "disciple indeed" comes through continuing in, and maturing in the knowledge of the Word of God. Unlike the "frozen chosen," a disciple or follower of Jesus will progress, will have action, will abound more and more. "*Now thanks be to God who always leads us into triumph in Christ, and through us diffuses the fragrance of His knowledge in every place*" (2 Cor. 2:14). You can't lead anyone anywhere if they are unwilling to move or step out. You are told to "*be doers of the word, and not hearers only, deceiving yourselves*" (James 1:22).

True saving faith will produce action. The love of Christ towards us is a compelling force. Our job is to stir ourselves up: to "*keep ourselves in the love of God*" (Jude 21). This, however, will come effortlessly when you make a decision to continue in His Word, and fellowship regularly with your heavenly Father. Ours is not a stagnant, dead faith, but a living faith where we go from faith to faith, and from glory to glory. "*I press toward the goal for the prize of the upward call of God in Christ Jesus*" (Phil. 3:14).

I challenge you "*to examine yourself as to whether or not you are in the faith. Test yourselves. Do you not know yourselves, that Jesus Christ is in you?*" (2

Cor. 13:5). When was the last time you stepped out in faith to a point where the supernatural power of God **had** to show up? When you decide to follow the prompting of the Holy Spirit or take a firm stand on the Word of God, you are in an exciting place! I have found a simple way for us to test ourselves and show ourselves where we are in our walk with God. "*And since we have the same spirit of faith, according to what is written, 'I believed and therefore I spoke, we also believe and therefore speak'*" (2 Cor. 4:13). When you truly believe the truths of God's Word, you will speak them. It is not enough to have heard a certain scripture, or be able to quote that scripture. You have to truly believe the scripture.

If you find yourself not speaking the Word of God over situations in your life, make sure you have more than just head knowledge of scripture. "*Death and life are in the power of the tongue, and those who love it will eat its fruit*" (Prov. 18:21). If you truly believed the power of the words you speak and the power of speaking God's Word, then you will be doing it. Also, it will be your number one "go to" and not a last resort. That is how you test yourself. The Bible says out of the abundance of your heart the mouth speaks. Whatever you are placing in your heart in abundance, is what you will be speaking.

There is a need in the world today for Christians to live a life of purpose, as burning and shining lights to reflect the glory of Christ. We must be sincere, because people can sense fake. When you are properly motivated by love, then you are sincere. Christians still have free will, and God will use you to the degree that you yield to Him. We ought to work towards complete surrender to the plan and will of God in our lives. You can never be totally sold out for God if you try to hold on to anything of your old natural life. As long as you hold on to the natural, you cannot take hold of divine life. *"But I press on, that I may lay hold of that which Christ Jesus has also laid hold of me"* (Phil. 3:12). Jesus came that we may have life, and have it more abundantly. We need to be ministers of that life, power, and healing virtue of Jesus Christ wherever we go. How? Yield, yield, yield. We must decrease so He can increase. Despite how it sounds, fully surrendering your life is not an act of weakness, but of great power.

We are called to be world flippers. *"These who have turned the world upside down have come here, too"* (Acts 17:16). Do you have a hard time seeing yourself as a world flipper? *"That the sharing of your faith may become effective by the acknowledgement of every good thing which is in you in Christ Jesus"* (Philem. 1:6). You must not identify yourself with who you are in the flesh—apart from Christ. Paul said, *"For I know that in me (that is, in my flesh) nothing good dwells..."* (Rom. 7:18). Instead, you must have your identity firmly rooted in who you are in the spirit—the real you. We must reject our emotions, the opinion of others, or anything else that does not line up with the Word of God concerning our identity. We must, however, believe that we are who God says we are. Study all of the "in Christ" and "in Him" scriptures until you have an accurate self image. Stamping out all condemnation and insecurity will position you to truly believe Eph. 3:20: "*Now to Him who is able to do exceedingly abundantly above all that we ask or think, according to the power that works **in us**.*" We've already been given everything we need to be more than conquerors through Jesus Christ our Lord.

Tag, you're it! This is exactly what Jesus was saying when He said, "*All authority has been given to Me in heaven and in earth. Go therefore and make disciples of all the nations...*" (Matt. 28:18–19). Will you continue the work? Will you grab the torch and run your race? I recognize that there are still some out there who think that only the apostles were commissioned with power. Let me show you this passage of scripture that includes every believer—from the least to the greatest. John chapter 17 records Jesus' intercessory prayer just before His arrest. He starts by confirming the eternal life given to all those that are with Him that believed in Him. He then speaks of their calling in verse 18. "*As You sent me into the world, I also have sent them into the world.*" God sent Jesus: powerful in word and deed. Likewise, Jesus sent His disciples into the world. Now, here is the good part. Verse 20 says, "*I do not pray for these alone, but also for those who will believe in Me through their word."* That is a direct reference to you individually, and the New Testament church as a whole. As God sent Jesus into the world, He is sending you into the world!

Christians are the only preserving element left in this fallen world. We truly are the salt of the earth. God saw it fitting to put His treasure into us—these earthen vessels. Let us go into all our world, or our sphere of influence, as fully yielded messengers of a loving God. What is our message? And what is our ministry? *"Now all things are of God, who has reconciled us to Himself through Jesus Christ, and has given us the ministry of reconciliation"* (2 Cor. 5:18). Now more than ever, ours is a ministry of reconciliation. *"That is, that God was in Christ reconciling the world to Himself, not imputing their trespasses to them, and has committed to us the word of reconciliation"* (2 Cor. 5:19).

Our mission is clear; we need to send out this message: The wrath of God toward man's sinfulness has been appeased through the offering of His Son Jesus Christ. He's not mad at you, He loves you and wants you to receive His forgiveness and enter into eternal life to forever be with Him. Verse 20 says quite plainly, *"Now then, we are ambassadors for Christ, as though God were pleading through us: we implore you on Christ's behalf, be reconciled to God."* The harvest is great, but the laborers are few. The God of love is not willing that any should perish. Listen to the cry of His heart, and let His love flow through you to reach a lost and dying world. Is there not a cause to live a life of purpose? "*Behold, now is the accepted time; behold, now is the day of salvation*" (2 Cor. 6:2). It is time for us to reveal the true character and nature of God to the world!

Chapter 8
Family

God values family and relationships. He sees children as "*a heritage from the Lord, and the fruit of the womb as a reward*" (Ps. 127:3). His attitude towards His children was reflected when Jesus said, "*Let the little children come to Me, and do not forbid them; for such is the kingdom of God*" (Mark 10:14). God wants us to seek Him, find Him, and draw near to Him. "*That they may all be one, as You, Father, are in Me, and I in You; that they also may be one in Us, that the world may believe that You sent Me*" (John 17:21). Uniting the family was one of the main objectives of Jesus' ministry. Before crucifixion he was able to say, "*I have glorified You on earth. I have finished the work which you have given Me to do*" (John 17:14). When I say "uniting the family," I am referring to the heavenly family not earthly families. Jesus' stance on this matter was clear when He said, "*'Who is my mother and who are my brothers?' And He stretched out His hand toward His disciples and said, 'Here are my mother and My brothers!'*" (Matt. 12:48–49). As far as our earthly families are concerned, the gospel can cause great division. Not everyone will accept the truth, and this can "*set a man against his father, a daughter against her mother... and a man's enemies will be that of his own household*" (Matt. 10:35–36). Thank God that we have been brought near by the blood of Jesus to a new family, a heavenly family.

Your position in this heavenly family can only be obtained by faith. "*For you are all sons of God through faith in Christ Jesus* (Gal. 3:26). Under the old covenant, only the Jews could claim this divine family linage. However, God "*predestined us to adoption as sons by Jesus Christ to Himself according to the good pleasure of His will*" (Eph. 1:5). Under the new covenant we have been adopted into the family; therefore, Jesus "*created in Himself one new man from the two, making peace, and that He might reconcile them both to God in one body through the cross ...*" (Eph. 2:15–16). This unity, this oneness, was the ultimate plan of God's redemption of mankind. "*Now, there is neither Jew nor Greek, there is neither slave nor free, there is neither male nor female; for you are all one in Christ Jesus*" (Gal. 3:28). If all the Jews had received Jesus with open arms, the rest of us, the Gentiles, would have been hung out to dry, so to speak. Instead, "*blindness in part has happened to Israel until the fullness of the Gentiles has come in*" (Rom. 11:25). Now we can clearly see that God is not willing that any should perish, but that all should come to repentance.

There is so much strength in a family that is united in Christ. The very gates of hell cannot prevail against a family that is holding fast to the head which is Christ. Even within the family, God has set up a system for His divine flow. Sometimes, political correctness, or new "enlightened" thinking causes problems in the family. *"But I want you to know that the head of every man is Christ, the head of woman is man, and the head of Christ is God"* (1 Cor. 11:3). God's plan for authority in the house is this: Christ—husband—wife—children. Notice that it is essential for the husband to follow Christ; to submit to His Lordship. When the husband has a healthy relationship with Jesus, he will almost automatically love his wife as Christ loved the church. He will be led by the Spirit and lead his family accordingly. The wife should willingly follow his leadership and authority. The children should respond to this respectful unity and follow their parents, who are following Christ. This may sound over simplified or unobtainable to some people.

You might be thinking, "You don't know my husband," or "You don't know my wife." You're right, I don't, but I do know this: our enemy will launch vicious attacks to disrupt the unity of a husband and wife. He knows the power of two walking together in agreement. *"Again I say to you that if two of you agree on earth concerning anything that they ask, it will be done for them by My father in heaven"* (Matt. 18:19). The Bible warns us not to be ignorant of Satan's devices. We must recognize when there's an attack on our marriage, look past the surface and see it for what it really is. If Satan can divide a wedge between a husband and wife, this will distract them from fulfilling their calling by forcing them to take their focus off of God and keep it on earthly things. Let's not give place to the devil. Men, love your wives. Women, respect your husbands. By doing this, you are allowing God's plan to function in your marriage and your family.

In addition to having a unified family, having a local church to call home has many benefits. *"And let us consider one another in order to stir up love and good works, not forsaking the assembling of ourselves together, as is the manner of some, but exhorting one another , and so much the more as you see the day approaching"* (Heb. 10:24–25). Many people go to church out of a sense of obligation or religious duty. Sadly, there are plenty of churches out there that will be obliged to help you scratch that religious itch without bringing any real benefit to your life. *"Now in giving these instructions I do not praise you, since you come together not for the better, but for the worse"* (1 Cor. 11:17). Not every church that you drive by is coming together for good despite the oversized cross or overcrowded parking lot.

You must be careful who you let speak into your life. It is all too easy to find a church that is subtly corrupting the minds of believers by straying from the Word of God and preaching a perverted gospel. The real harm is done when the people go out and spread their twisted or powerless "gospel" that gives others a distorted image of God that is contrary to His Word. It is important to find a Bible-believing, and therefore Spirit-filled church that is bearing fruit. Attending the wrong church and believing their wrong doctrine can literally cut short your life here on earth. We need to become like the people Paul ministered to in Acts chapter 17, "*in that they received the word with all readiness and searched the scripture daily to find out whether these things were so*" (Acts. 17:11). We must let the Bible be the final authority, even if that means leaving your current church. The same way faith comes by hearing, so does fear, doubt, and unbelief. Therefore, you can't keep sitting under false doctrine and wrong teaching without it creeping into your mind and affecting your heart. This is why we are told to "*guard our hearts with all diligence*" (Prov. 4:23).

Like I mentioned before, we live in a fallen world and also have an enemy who is trying to bring destruction to our lives. Sooner or later you will encounter an attack against your physical body. It would be a very sad thing to be attending a church that doesn't believe it is God's will for all to be healed. "*Is anyone among you sick? Let him call for the elders of the church, and let them pray over him, anointing him with oil in the name of the Lord. And the prayer of faith shall save the sick, and the Lord will raise him up"* (James 5: 14–15). If your pastor is not confident in ministering the healing power found in the name of Jesus, well ... good luck with that. A church's beliefs are more important than all their programs, production value, or "cool" factor. In times of great trial, you'd better be part of a church that takes a firm stand on the Word of God, and is being led by His Spirit.

So what exactly are the benefits of being plugged into a good local church? *"From who the whole body, joined and knit together by what every joint supplies, according to the effective working by which every part does its share, causes growth of the body for the edifying of itself in love"* (Eph. 4:16). Church should be the place we come to be built up and encouraged. We need to learn who we are, what we have, and how to use it. Church is *"for the equipping of the saints for the work of the ministry, for the edifying of the body of Christ"* (Eph. 4:12). We come to have spiritual truths imparted to us, so that we can be built up before being sent out. Basically, one of the main reasons we go to church should be to learn. *"Grace and peace be multiplied to you in the knowledge of God and of Jesus our Lord"* (2 Peter 1:2). Once again, this is why it is so important to be sitting under preaching and teaching that exalts the finished work of Jesus Christ. God said, *"My people perish for lack of knowledge*" (Hos. 4:6, KJV), and we know that in Christ are hidden all the treasures of wisdom and knowledge. Therefore, people perish for a lack of knowing Jesus and the totality of His sacrifice for us.

We should also attend church to reap the benefits of corporate worship and fellowship. The Holy Spirit was given at Pentecost when the believers were in one place and in one accord. Paul exhorts the churches over and over again to be of one mind, and pursue unity. Jesus said, "*For where two or three are gathered together in My name, I am there in the midst of them*" (Matt. 18:20). There is also an element of safety that comes with building real relationships with like-minded believers. "*Where there is no council, the people fall; but in the multitude of counselors there is safety*" (Prov. 11:14). Our enemy wants nothing more than to isolate a believer, making them an easier target for attack.

Finally, we go to minister the gifts we've been given, as well as receive from others. "*But now God has set the members, each one of them, in the body just as He pleased*" (1 Cor. 12:18). We are the body of Christ, and members individually. Your specific gifting can be a blessing in another member's life, and in turn, theirs can bless your life. It is just as important to have "inreach," or the building up of the members, as it is to have effective outreach. When it comes to advancing the kingdom of God, what could be more effective than having likeminded co-laborers? "*Two are better than one, because they have a good reward for their labor. For if they fall, one will lift up his companion"* (Eccl. 4:9–10). The local church can be a powerful and effective force that uses each member's gifts and talents for the furtherance of the Gospel.

At the beginning of this book, I spoke of the need for unity of the body of Christ today. I believe much of the disunity we see is caused by a lack of knowledge pertaining to the true character and nature of God. He truly has become "the God they worship without knowing." A strong active relationship with Him will allow you to quickly recognize false statements about Him. *"That we should no longer be children, tossed to and fro and carried be every wind of doctrine, by the trickery of men, in the cunning craftiness of deceitful plotting..."* (Eph. 4:14). We need to be accurate witnesses that give a true testimony of our God to the world. While the religious Pharisees spread the message of condemnation and self-righteousness, let us spread God's message of love, grace, and forgiveness. *"Behold, let us love one another, for love is of God; and everyone who loves is born of God and knows God. He who does not have love does not know God, for God is love"* (1 John 4:7–8).

Jesus said two times in John chapter 17 that perfect unity or oneness of the body would help the world to know that God had sent Him. This book has been an attempt to reveal the Biblically accurate version of God.

It is my hope that it will challenge personal beliefs, and expose the lies of the enemy that have crept into our churches. I hope I have explained the many benefits of knowing God, and the value we should place on our personal relationship with Him. I want the body to know that by the blood of Jesus, they are worthy to draw near to God. Above all, He desires and longs for closeness with you as His beloved son or daughter with whom He is well pleased. I believe if we would pursue this oneness, divisions would decrease and unity would increase.

Let's endeavor to become the united church that takes the gospel to the ends of the earth. Let's go out motivated by love and empowered by the Holy Spirit. Won't you help reveal the unknown God? I leave you with one last passage of scripture: "*And we know that the Son of God has come and has given us an understanding, that we may know Him who is true; and we are in Him who is true, in His Son Jesus Christ. This is the true God and eternal life*" (1 John 5:20).

Prayer to Receive Salvation

My friends, you have heard the true gospel by reading this book. Choosing to receive this great and awesome gift from God is the most important decision you will ever make! His Word promises, *"That if you confess with your mouth the Lord Jesus and believe in your heart that God has raised Him from the dead, you will be saved. For with the heart one believes unto righteousness, and with the mouth confession is made unto salvation"* (Rom. 10:9–10). For whoever calls on the name of the Lord shall be saved (Rom. 10:13).

By His grace, God has already done everything to provide salvation. Your part is to believe and receive. Pray this out loud: "Jesus, I confess that you are my Lord and Savior. I believe in my heart that God raised You from the dead. By faith in Your Word, I receive salvation now. Thank You for saving me!"

The very moment you commit your life to Jesus Christ, the truth of His Word instantly comes to pass in your spirit. Now you are born again; you are a brand new creation!

Prayer to Receive the Baptism of the Holy Spirit

Most of the people that I know who've received the baptism of the Holy Spirit received it while a Spirit-filled believer laid hands on them. However, it doesn't have to come that way. As His child, your loving heavenly Father wants to give you the supernatural power you need to live this new life. *"For everyone who asks receives, and he who seeks finds, and to him who knocks it will be opened ... how much more will your heavenly Father give the Holy Spirit to those who ask Him?"*
All you have to do is ask, believe, and receive. Pray this: "Father, I recognize my need for Your power to live this new life. Please fill me with Your Holy Spirit. By faith I receive it right now! Holy Spirit, You are welcome in my life! Thank You for baptizing me!" Some syllables from a language you don't recognize will rise up from your heart to your mouth. Begin to speak them out loud by faith.

Remember, it doesn't matter whether or not you "felt" anything spectacular. If you believed in your heart that you received, then God's Word promises you did! *"Therefore I say to you, whatever things you ask when you pray, believe that you receive them, and you will have them"* (Mark 11:24). God always honors His Word; believe it! Let me be the first to congratulate you. Now you are filled with God's supernatural power! When you pray with tongues, you are releasing God's power from within and building yourself up in the spirit (1 Cor. 14:4). You can do this whenever you like. Enjoy this refreshing. Enjoy this gift from the Father!

www.ingramcontent.com/pod-product-compliance
Lightning Source LLC
Chambersburg PA
CBHW060358050426
42449CB00009B/1792